WALKING, CYCLING ~ ~~~~~
ALONG THE WIRR~
and
THE STORY OF
HOOTON TO WEST KIRB~
By Ian & Marilyn Bou~~~~~~~y

Design & Origination
Ian Boumphrey - Desktop Publisher
Additional Work - John Boumphrey

Artwork - Philippa Gordon-Smith

Printed by
Eaton Press
Westfield Road
Wallasey
Merseyside L44 7JB

Published by
Ian & Marilyn Boumphrey
"The Nook" 7 Acrefield Road
Prenton Wirral L42 8LD
Tel/Fax: 0151 608 7611
e-mail: ianb@wirralpc.u-net.com
http:/www.io-ltd.com/yw

ISBN 1-899241-06-X

Front Cover Photographs:
Hadlow Road Station, Willaston
[Cheshire County Council, Countryside Management Service].
The Old Station Platform at Thurstaston
[Martyn Jamieson]

1

**Price
£2.99**

INTRODUCTION

No publication about the Wirral Way would be complete without the story of the Hooton to West Kirby Railway. So we have combined a guide, giving information to walkers, cyclists and horse riders, with a history of the railway together with photographs of the old stations. There is a list of useful addresses and telephone numbers on page 25.

HOW TO USE THE GUIDE

Turn to the centre pages which have an artist-drawn map of Wirral showing the route taken by the Wirral Way and its access points. It also gives details of parking, information boards, picnic sites, toilets etc.

The access points listed and numbered on the right and page numbers underneath them refer to those on the map and the relevant pages in the book e.g. access point number 5 on the right refers to "Croft Drive, Caldy (see pages 7/9)". On the map this shows that the facilities there include parking, information board and picnic site. If the reader wants further information then, turning to page 7, there is the walk to Croft Drive from Sandy Lane bridge and page 9 is from Croft Drive to Thurstaston.

The walks are all listed on odd numbered pages on the right and the story of the railway, together with photographs of the old stations, are on even numbers on the left.

Occasionally the footpath and horse/cyclists routes are swapped over and at the time this guide went to press there was a possibility that the section between Caldy/Thurstaston would be changed over - check signs.

If you want an update of further information contact the relevant addresses or telephone numbers on page 25.

WALKERS:

Being a converted railway line, the Wirral Way is mostly flat. However, walking boots, although not essential, are recommended - or wellingtons, after rainy periods, when the paths could be muddy or waterlogged. Walkers are advised to keep to their designated footpaths watching out for cyclists (on the Wirral Borough Council part of the way) and horse riders.

Plan your route - especially if relying on public transport.

RAILWAY: There are Merseyrail stations at West Kirby and Hooton with other railway connections also at Hooton and at Neston.
For details of timetables etc. refer to the contact telephone numbers on page 25.

BUSES: There are several bus connections along the Wirral Way and at the time of going to press these include: the centre of West Kirby; Thurstaston on the A540 (about a mile from the visitor centre); Lower Village, Heswall; Parkgate promenade; Neston; Willaston and Hooton. Plan your route and as many of these services are infrequent - **check on timetables** - there are relevant telephone numbers on page 25.

One of the attractions of the Wirral Way is that many circular walks can be incorporated by exploring sidetracks, pathways and connecting lanes using bus stops or car parks along the way. Some of these are included in booklets available from the Thurstaston Visitor Centre and for the more adventurous who want to explore the quiet paths and byways there are Ordnance Survey Maps.

CYCLISTS:
At present cycling is only allowed on the part of the Wirral Way managed by Wirral Borough Council - from Church Road, West Kirby up to the Heswall/Neston border.

Cycling is not allowed on the footpath. Where permitted to ride, the cyclists must keep to their track - which they share with horse riders. So be aware, look out for horse riders and also walkers, especially where the two tracks merge.

Cycling along the Wirral Way within Cheshire:
An exciting new project - The National Cycle Route - is proposed to run in part along the Wirral Way within Cheshire. Cheshire County Council are considering this at present, as a means of upgrading the Wirral Way within its area so as to provide for safe, family cycling. It is hoped that work would start in 1996/97.

At the time of printing, cycling has not been safely integrated onto the Wirral Way within Cheshire. Cyclists are therefore asked to cycle only in permitted areas.
For up to the minute information please telephone:
**Cheshire County Council, Countryside Management Service
at Willaston on: 0151 327 5145/2084**
before planning your route. Thank you.

HORSE RIDERS:
Horse riders have use of their own track for most of the Wirral Way from Church Road, West Kirby - which they share with cyclists on the Wirral Borough Council side up to the Heswall/Neston border - to Church Lane, Neston, then from Mellock Lane through to Heath Lane, Willaston.

WEST KIRBY JOINT STATION - Opened 19 April 1886

West Kirby Joint Station, which opened 19 April 1886, was the terminus when the Hooton to Parkgate line was extended to West Kirby. A turntable was used to turn the engines for the return journey.

The main station at West Kirby had opened in 1878 when the Birkenhead to Hoylake line, which had opened in 1866, was extended to West Kirby. The present station building, which is the terminus for the Merseyrail Wirral Line, was opened in 1896. The concrete platform canopies were added in 1938 when the line was electrified

Although the Wirral Railway and the Joint Company failed to agree on building one central station, a spur line connected the two systems and was used by both goods and passenger trains. From October 1923, the spur line was used for a through passenger service which was introduced from New Brighton to London Euston.

The line was closed to passengers 15 September 1956 and finally to goods 7 May 1962. The track was taken up from March 1964.

West Kirby Concourse was built in 1970 on land between the two stations and the bridge which had carried Grange Road over the railway was demolished in 1980 and the road widened.

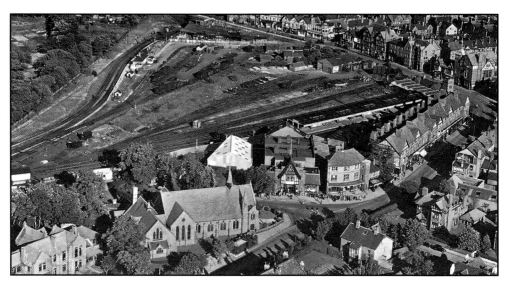

This aerial view of West Kirby, which was taken c.1958, shows the Hooton/West Kirby spur line and West Kirby Joint Railway Station top left. The other side of Grange Road, under which this spur line disappears, is now the start of the Wirral Way. The nearest of the railway lines leads to the main West Kirby Station, which can be seen behind the black and white Tudor Cinema in the centre of the picture.

4

WALKING FROM THE CENTRE OF WEST KIRBY TO SANDY LANE, WEST KIRBY

The starting point at the West Kirby end of the Wirral Way is West Kirby Station. From the front of the station, cross over Grange Road and turning left you will pass the Dee Hotel, Westbourne Road and the entrance to the Wirral Country Park is a further 50 metres on the right.

If you are proceeding downhill into West Kirby, pass the church on the left, then Brookfield Road and the access point is 50 metres beyond on the left.

The Wirral Way follows the site of the old railway line and even in this urban setting there is an abundance of wildlife. Look out for the black caps, willow warblers, chiff chaffs etc. After a short distance, the first of several entrances to Ashton Park is passed; then under the footbridge connecting both parts of the park before reaching Church Road Bridge. This is the first of many over-bridges between here and Parkgate built of brick when this part of the line was opened in 1886. However, beyond Parkgate the bridges, which were erected by 1866, were built of sandstone. Access to Church Road is on both sides, with St Bridget's Churchyard and Church seen on the left. Beyond the bridge is where cyclists and horse riders join the Wirral Way keeping to the right where the track splits with walkers to the left. Kirby Park Station was originally sited on the left before reaching Sandy Lane bridge, where access to West Kirby Village, with the *Moby Dick* pub and Post Office, to the left and West Kirby Sailing Club and Marine Lake to the right.

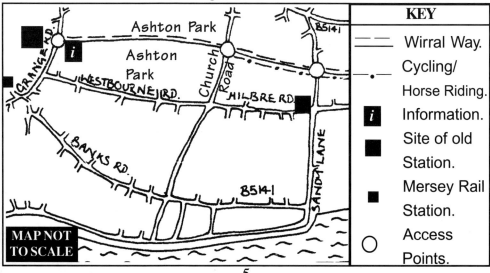

KEY	
‒ ‒ ‒	Wirral Way.
‒ • ‒	Cycling/ Horse Riding.
i	Information.
■	Site of old Station.
■	Mersey Rail Station.
○	Access Points.

MAP NOT TO SCALE

KIRBY PARK STATION - Opened October 1894

The view below, taken from Sandy Lane bridge, of Kirby Park's small station and platform, which can be seen to the right of the track, was on a postcard sent in August 1909. To the right of Church Road bridge in the distance can be seen St Bridget's School and Church tower. The flagpole, which can be seen further to the right, is standing in the grounds of the West Kirby Hotel. This stood in Village Road until it was demolished in 1964, when it was replaced by the Moby Dick. The column on Caldy Hill is clearly visible in the top right corner of the picture.

The station was closed to passengers in July 1954 but the coal siding to the left remained in use until the line finally closed in 1962. This scene has totally changed as most of the land on both sides of the railway line has been developed for housing.

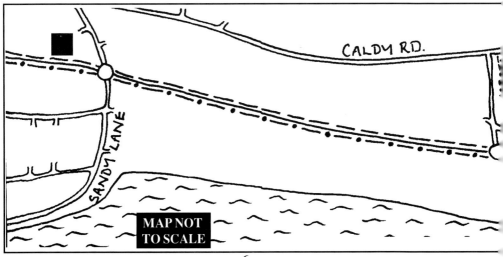

6

WALKING FROM SANDY LANE BRIDGE TO CALDY

The first view of the River Dee and Welsh Hills beyond is on the right and here there is a footpath with access to the shore south of West Kirby Sailing Club and Marine Lake, both of which can be seen to the right.

Looking to the left can be seen boats moored off Dee Sailing Club at Thurstaston. There is also a coastal path here running parallel with the Wirral Way. Part of Caldy Hill can be seen inland. A short distance, further along the Wirral Way, on the right by a wooden bridge is a wonderful view over the River Dee.

Melloncroft Drive access point is soon reached where a short walk up Melloncroft Drive on the left leads to Caldy Hill, National Trust land, which is the other side of Caldy Road. Cubbins Green is to the right of the Wirral Way and there is access to the coastal path which goes along the banks of the River Dee. However, the only way through part of this path is via the shore.

Continuing on, the picnic benches, information board and car park are soon reached [NOTE that the car park closes here at dusk].

The old station was sited before reaching Croft Drive. Turning left here leads to Caldy Village, right to Caldy shore or cross over Croft Drive to rejoin the Wirral Way (continued on page 9).

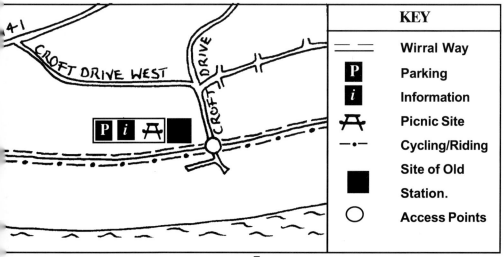

KEY	
= = =	Wirral Way
P	Parking
i	Information
⛱	Picnic Site
—•—	Cycling/Riding
◼	Site of Old Station.
○	Access Points

CALDY STATION - Opened May 1909

This is a postcard view of Caldy Station sent to Joe Ellams, station master at Kirby Park Station, from the station master of Caldy Station, shortly after it was opened in May 1909. The proof that this corrugated iron building was Caldy Station is the name Caldy on the seat and also on the lamp to the right of the station master. The ladies' waiting room is to the left and the booking office to the right.

This station was closed by British Railways in the February 1954 closure programme.

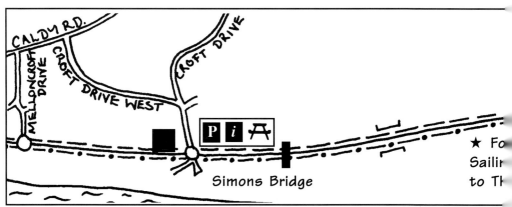

WALKING FROM CALDY TO THURSTASTON

Just after the access point from Croft Drive, travelling south, the Wirral Way splits with walkers to the right and cyclists and horse riders to the left. [NOTE that as this booklet went to press, there was a possibility that the footpath and horse/cyclist routes along this section would be swapped over - check the signs!]. The path passes under Simon's Bridge then Caldy Golf Club course can be seen either side with their club house in the distance on the left. A footpath on the right, opposite a sign "Beware of Horses", leads to Dee Sailing Club and gives access to Thurstaston shore. The roadway here leads to Station Road and the Thurstaston Visitor's Centre.

Back on the Wirral Way, the spire of Thurstaston Church is seen in the distance to the right of Thurstaston Hill which is on the left horizon. Some distance on, the access road to Dee Sailing Club is on the right and then on the same side the entrance can be seen to the Thurstaston Caravan Park.

Before the path passes under the Station Road bridge there is a sign for Toilets which are up some steps. The Visitor's Centre can be reached beyond the toilets, across Station Road, turn right and through a gap in the hedge on the left.

Alternatively, the Visitor's Centre can be reached by going under the bridge, alongside the original platform, following the sign up the steps to the right and along the path to the centre. For details of the Thurstaston Visitor's Centre see page 11.

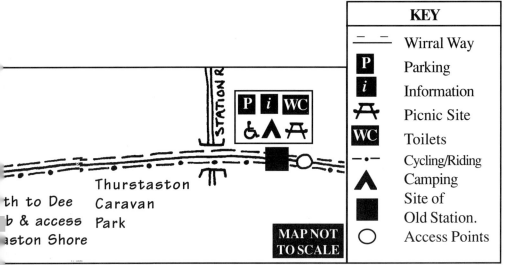

KEY	
——	Wirral Way
P	Parking
i	Information
⊼	Picnic Site
WC	Toilets
-·-	Cycling/Riding
▲	Camping
■	Site of Old Station.
○	Access Points

Thurstaston Caravan Park

th to Dee
b & access
aston Shore

MAP NOT TO SCALE

THURSTASTON STATION - Opened April 1886

Thurstaston Station was opened when the line was extended from Parkgate to West Kirby in April 1886. Originally the line was to have passed closer to Thurstaston Village, but, Thomas Ismay, the owner of the large house "Dawpool" at Thurstaston and Chairman of the railway company, instigated the rerouting of the line nearer to the River Dee, keeping the noise and smoke away from his residence. He was also the founder of the White Star Line - of Titanic fame.

The main station building was erected on the landward side of the platform, and can be seen in the photograph below, with four railway cottages behind (the station master's house is out of view to the left). Part of the land on the river side of the platform was acquired by Lever Brothers in 1919 and by 1921 they had opened Thurstaston Camp for the benefit of their employees. The camp was in use until the outbreak of war in 1939 and from 1941 the site was used by an anti-aircraft battery as part of Merseyside's defences. Some of the concrete buildings are now buried under the grassed mounds between the Visitor's Centre and the cliffs.

Thurstaston Station closed in February 1954 at the same time as Caldy Station and, together with Hadlow Road Station, is now one of only two platforms preserved on this former line.

THURSTASTON VISITOR CENTRE

The Thurstaston Visitor Centre, which was opened in 1973 as the focal point for Britain's first Country Park, is now run by Wirral Borough Council's Leisure Services & Tourism Dept.

The centre is open all year round and its facilities include:-

An information and sales desk where you can find out what's on, pick up free leaflets or purchase books and pamphlets on trails and walks around Thurstaston and other areas in the Wirral peninsula, also on local history and wildlife. Postcards, videos, maps, tide tables, souvenirs etc. are also on sale.

A Lecture Theatre where there are regular talks on a variety of subjects; fascinating exhibitions, video and audiovisual slide shows that tell the story of the park. Outside there is a refreshment kiosk, plenty of areas to picnic, a barbecue site, campsite, cafe and shop.

All this and the hedgerows, ponds and shore to explore for wildlife and flowers. Look for the excellent *Wirral Country Park Official Trail Map & Guide* for sale in the Visitor's Centre.

The Wirral Park Rangers

It is the Rangers that make sure most of these facilities are available to the public, and they can be recognised by their distinctive green uniform. Besides always being ready to answer questions, the Rangers' duties also include giving talks, guided walks and bike rides to both children and adults throughout the year; laying hedges, planting shrubs and trees, and keeping vegetation under control; organising a wildlife rehabilitation centre and exercising a general supervision over the country park.

Each year some 18,000 school children visit the centre and many take part in Ranger-led activities - pond dips, seashore search, bug hunts etc.

If you want further information on any of the services offered, contact:-
Thurstaston Visitor Centre, Wirral Country Park, Station Road, Thurstaston, Wirral L61 0HN Tel: 0151 648 4371 or 3884
or: Director of Leisure Services and Tourism, Westminster House, Hamilton Street, Birkenhead, Wirral Tel: 0151 647 2366

The station master, Bill Doig, on the far platform between the engines' chimneys, can be seen surveying the damage caused by a head-on collision at Thurstaston Station on Monday 25 February 1957. Even though the single line was working on a "foolproof system" to avoid accidents, this had obviously not worked on this occasion. The train from West Kirby, pictured left, struck the stationary ex LMS "Jinty" 0-6-0 engine head-on. The two engines and four wagons were derailed, luckily without major injury to the railway staff.

This map shows the route taken by the Wirral Way together with its access points. All the parking areas shown are free except Hooton, where there is only a nominal charge (25p at time of publishing). Parking in the centre of West Kirby can be expensive and is not advised.

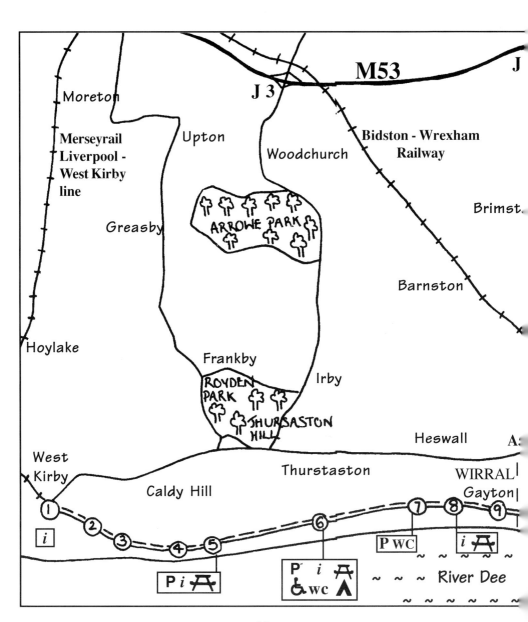

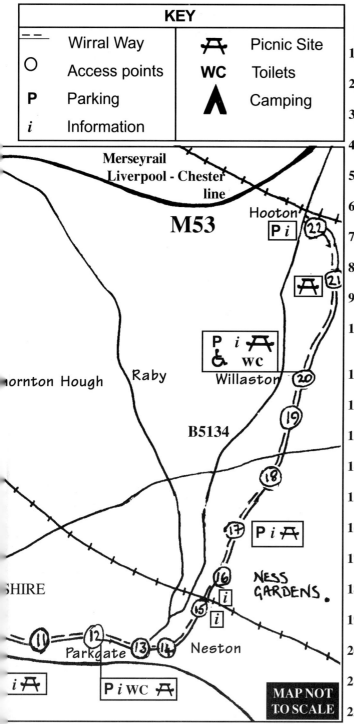

KEY

– –	Wirral Way	🔝	Picnic Site
O	Access points	WC	Toilets
P	Parking	⋀	Camping
i	Information		

Merseyrail
Liverpool - Chester
line

M53

Hooton

P i ㉒

🔝 ㉑

P i 🔝
♿ WC

ornton Hough   Raby   Willaston ⑳

B5134

⑲

⑱

⑰ P i 🔝

⑯ NESS
GARDENS •
i

SHIRE ⑮ i

⑪ ⑫ ⑬ ⑭ Neston
Parkgate

i 🔝

P i WC 🔝

MAP NOT
TO SCALE

HESWALL STATION - Opened 19 April 1886

Access to the paved platforms was via the booking office (the building with the clock) in Station Road and down the steps which can be seen either side of the incoming train from Thurstaston. All the railway buildings were brick-built except the wooden signal box and the only ones standing today are the station master's house and four railway cottages. The station closed to passengers in 1956 and to goods in 1962. The British Railways Board sold an eight acre site for housing, including the station and goods yard fronting onto Davenport Road, in 1966 for £30,250. Riverbank Close now occupies the site of the station.

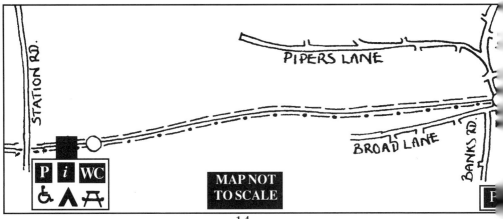

WALKING FROM THURSTASTON TO RIVERBANK ROAD HESWALL

When leaving Thurstaston, cyclists and horse riders keep to the left and walkers follow the signs which take them to the right of the barbecue area. After a short distance the path runs parallel to the horse and cycle track, then crossing over it, the camp site can be seen on the left.

Between here and Heswall there are many chances to see the wonderful view across the River Dee to the Welsh hills beyond.

On the left can be seen the spire of Thurstaston Church. The Dungeon Bridge is also on the left and after a bench on the right there is a sign for the Dungeon (a local term for a dell) which is the wooded area viewed on the left. This was once said to be the haunt of smugglers.

The boundary stone between the Parish of St Bartholomew, Thurstaston and St Peter, Heswall is a few metres further along on the right and after a short distance is a seat in memory of Mrs Mary Bicknell.

The first of two signs to the right for Heswall Fields and Beach is soon reached and walkers have to be wary when crossing the cycle and horse path. The straight tree-lined stretch here is a popular place for rabbits.

A footpath on the left, where the walker has to duck under a barrier, leads to Pipers Lane. Market gardens can be seen to the right then after some distance a sign points to Banks Road where there is a shop selling snacks, drinks, ice cream etc.; a bus stop and toilets 200 yds down Banks Road.

The path passes firstly under Delavor Road bridge then Farr Hall Drive bridge and joining Davenport Road for 1/3 mile where the houses on the left were built on the site of the railway line. Station Road on the left leads up to Lower Heswall village where there are shops and two pubs. The next road on the left, Riverbank Close, is the site of the former Heswall Station.

The Wirral Way footpath is then signposted on the left.

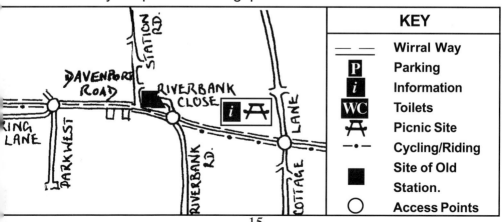

KEY	
— —	Wirral Way
P	Parking
i	Information
WC	Toilets
⛬	Picnic Site
–·–	Cycling/Riding
■	Site of Old Station.
○	Access Points

PARKGATE STATION - Opened 19 April 1866

Parkgate Station was the terminus for the Hooton to Parkgate line which opened 19 April 1866. When the extension to West Kirby was opened in 1886, the station at Parkgate was moved from the south to the north side of Station Road. The new station, seen here in 1906, had two wooden buildings with canopies either side of the line and were linked by subway. The site of the old station was developed as a goods yard with most of the trade coming from the Wirral Colliery. Fresh fish from Parkgate was also an important local trade carried by the railway. The station closed to passengers in 1956 and goods in 1962. The bridge over Station Road was removed in 1965 and has not been replaced.

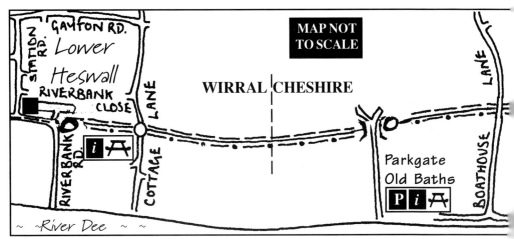

WALKING from RIVERBANK ROAD, HESWALL to STATION ROAD, PARKGATE

Access is down Station Road, turn left at the end (or along Davenport Road past the bottom of Station Road) then past Riverbank Close (the site of Heswall Station) and the Wirral Way footpath is signposted on the left. Walkers keep to the left of the picnic area and the cyclists/riders to the right. Pass under Cottage Lane bridge, where there is an access point to Cottage Lane. Heswall Golf Club House can be seen on the left beyond the golf course. Two benches face the River Dee and Welsh hills beyond as does another one a short distance further on. The Heswall Golf Course, which is private land, crosses the Wirral Way three times to holes on the Dee side of the Wirral Way and after the third one there is a stone on the left depicting the border between the Parish of St Peter's, Heswall and St Mary & St Helen, Neston. The next landmark is the Backwood Hall bridge, where there is an access point on the left to Backwood Hall Lane. This path leads towards the River Dee then turns left at the bottom and into the Parkgate Baths picnic site*. Back on the Wirral Way, at the Brooklands Road bridge there is an access point where the path off to the left leads to Wood Lane. Riders also leave here, following their signs which take them on to Station Road. Turning right at this access point leads to Brooklands Road and the promenade at Parkgate. The walkers cross the bridge and before reaching Station Road parts of the old Parkgate Station platform can be seen before the walkers' path turns to the left and descends to Station Road, Parkgate.

A popular circular walk is from the Parkgate Old Baths picnic site to Backwood Hall bridge then along the Wirral Way to Station Road, turn right, down to Parkgate front and, after an ice cream, continue along the promenade past the Boathouse Restaurant and back to the car park. This site overlooks the nature reserve of Gayton Sands and is an excellent place to observe the bird life of the Dee Estuary at its spectacular best.

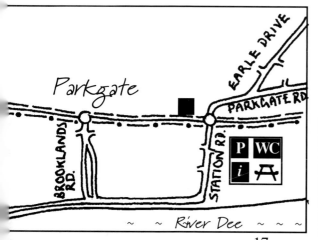

– – –	Wirral Way
P	Parking
i	Information
🛱	Picnic Site
WC	Toilets
– • –	Cycling/Riding
■	Site of Old Station.
○	Access Points

17

NESTON (SOUTH) STATION

Neston Station was opened at the same time as the line from Hooton to Parkgate, 1 October 1866. The other station at Neston, on the Bidston - Wrexham Line, which opened 18 May 1896, was initially known as Neston, then Neston & Parkgate, later Neston North (at the same time the station on the Hooton/West Kirby line was renamed Neston South) and today is known just as Neston. Neston South closed to passengers in 1956 and finally to goods in 1962. The land surrounding the station was bought for development by builders before the trackbed, which was to form the Country Park, was purchased by Cheshire County Council.

This 1965 view of Neston (South) Station shows the station master's house and other buildings overlooking the former, now overgrown, track prior to the land being sold to builders. The Mellock Lane bridge can be seen in the centre background with the houses in Station Road now occupying the site.

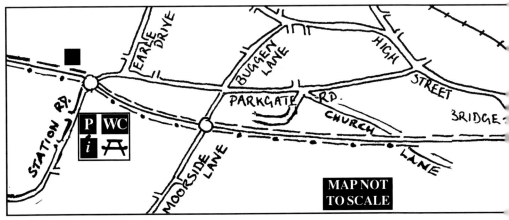

WALKING FROM STATION ROAD, PARKGATE TO NESTON

Access to the south bound Wirral Way is between where the railway bridge (now dismantled) crossed Station Road and the entrance to Neston Cricket Club. Turning into the path leading to the Wirral Way, the building on the right was once the station master's house, riders turn left and walkers keep straight on. At the top of the path, where the toilets are on the left, walkers keep to the right of the information board. Foxes can often be glimpsed crossing the picnic area soon reached on the left. It is here that the wildflower lords and ladies, so named because of its unusually shaped flower which has been connected with fertility rites since the middle ages, grows amongst the hawthorns. Upon reaching Moorside Lane bridge the access point to the lane is before the bridge on the left. During the Spring the smell of garlic from the wildflower, ramsons, fills the air - look on the left for its broad, flat leaves and white flowers. At the wooden barrier the walkers' path is to the left and the riders' to the right. After a short walk, the footpath off to the left is to Beechways, Neston and following the footpath to the right at this point, leads to Old Quay Lane. The next signpost on the right points to the * Old Quay and as this path crosses private land - keep to the footpath. Riders must leave the Wirral Way turning left to Church Lane, right to Eldon Terrace, left into Bridge Street and right at the mini roundabout (see below). Walkers keep straight on descending the steps at the bridge. It is at this point that the Wirral Way continues for a short distance by road. Turning left into Bridge Street, cross over at the mini roundabout, turning right into Station Road (DANGEROUS ROAD -CROSS WITH CAUTION). Past the information board and under the railway bridge there is a small children's play area on the left known as Stanney Fields. Keep along Station Road up to Mellock Lane. Cross over the road for the path leading onto the Wirral Way.

A short circular walk is possible here which takes the walker to the edge of the Dee Estuary saltmarsh and the Neston reed bed - dominated by common reed - Britain's tallest grass.

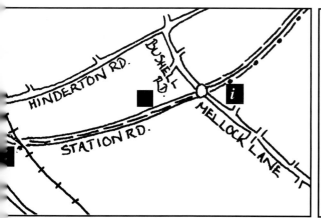

		Wirral Way
	P	Parking
	i	Information
	⛱	Picnic Site
	WC	Toilets
	—•—	Horse Riding
	■	Site of Old Station.
	○	Access Points

HADLOW ROAD STATION

The station, which opened in 1866, was called Hadlow Road Station so as not to confuse it with the Willaston near Crewe. This view of the station, which closed to passengers 17 September 1956, shows a train departing for West Kirby. The station is now a halt on the Wirral Way with the buildings beautifully preserved and the booking office looking as it would have done in 1952.

K E Y	— — Wirral Way	**P** Parking	■ Site of Old Station.
	WC Toilets	**i** Information	
	—•— Horse Riding	🛆 Picnic Site	○ Access Points

WALKING FROM MELLOCK LANE
NESTON TO HADLOW ROAD, WILLASTON

The access point is in Mellock Lane opposite Station Road where the path drops down into a deep rock cutting, past the information board. This half mile stretch, where the sun rarely reaches, abounds with a range of plants, wildlife and rocks. The first bridge (with a number six on the side) was built to carry cattle and farm vehicles. Just past here on the right is the date 1866 (when the line opened). Under the next bridge, where Lees Lane crosses over the Wirral Way, the land opens up as the cutting is left behind and the Lees Lane picnic area, and car park with information board, is on the left. The ponds here are old marl pits. At the gate, where walkers go ahead, riders keep to the left, rejoining the way at Cuckoo Lane. Before the wooden bridge crosses over Cuckoo Lane there is a sign on the right for a path to Little Neston and beyond is an old railway gradient post. The path is dual-use from Cuckoo Lane to just beyond Damhead Lane. As the Chester High Road (A540) bridge approaches, the path runs parallel with the road leading to the Liverpool University Veterinary Centre where a sign asks walkers to keep their animals under control. Keep a look out here for rabbits, with warrens on the left and beyond the road bridge on the right. There is an access point under the next bridge on the right at Damhead Lane. A public footpath crosses the Wirral Way after a short distance leading on the right to the Chester High Road and a bit further on, to Willaston on the left. The white crossing gates at Hadlow Road Station are soon reached. Access for the walkers and riders to the station is across the road - BEWARE OF TRAFFIC. The toilets are accessed through the ticket office on the platform. It is here where the office can be seen in a time capsule of 1952. To continue along the Wirral Way, walkers pass to the left of the signal box and through the car park [NOTE the car park closes at various times - see information board]. The date 1866 is seen above the entrance to the waiting room from the car park.

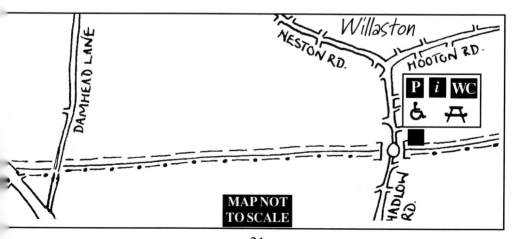

21

HOOTON STATION

This view of Hooton Station, which had opened on the Birkenhead to Chester line on 22 September 1840, is looking towards Birkenhead. The branch line to Parkgate was opened on 1 October 1866 and In 1886 the line was extended to West Kirby. This line closed to passengers in 1956 and to goods in 1962. The West Kirby branch trains used the extreme left hand side platform where the trees are growing today.

Hooton Station.

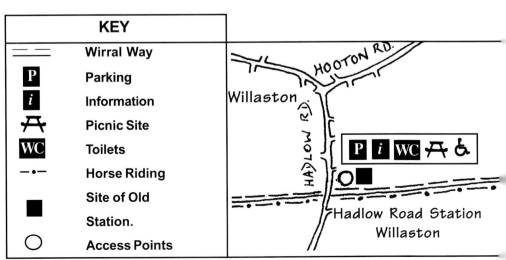

KEY	
— —	**Wirral Way**
P	**Parking**
i	**Information**
🛆	**Picnic Site**
WC	**Toilets**
—•—	**Horse Riding**
■	**Site of Old Station.**
○	**Access Points**

WALKING FROM HADLOW ROAD, WILLASTON TO HOOTON

Hadlow Road Station is the base of Cheshire County Council Countryside Management on Wirral Country Park. The waiting room/ticket office is open 9am to 5pm every day (except Christmas Day). The small display within the station master's house has occasional opening but can be opened on request or by arrangement - telephone number on page 25.

Walkers leave Hadlow Road Station platform by turning left at the signal box, turn right and join the Wirral Way at the far end of the car park [NOTE the car park closes at various times - see information board]. Along the way there is a sign to a farm on the left where, when open, eggs can be bought and the public are invited to view the pigs and hens. The footpath crosses over the riders' way and then straight on to Heath Lane, which can be reached by turning left at the end of the path. Riders must leave the Wirral Way here or continue on under Heath Lane bridge (note the old railway gradient post) taking the path to the right. A short distance after the path, on the same side, is a picnic area. On certain summer nights the glow-worm, with its biochemical light, can be observed along this stretch of the Wirral Way - surely one of nature's marvels. The path continues on eventually bending round to the left when the Hooton Industrial Estate is reached, with the area on the left being known as the Roften works, and the railway appears on the right. At the end of the Wirral Way take the ramp beyond the information board up to Hooton Road, turn right and walk over the bridge. The steps lead down to Hooton Station where there is access to British Rail and Merseyrail. There is an excellent, fully stocked, licensed shop for all requirements and beyond that is a car park where there is a nominal charge (25p at time of publishing).

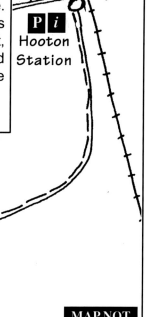

Hooton Road

P *i*

Hooton
Station

MAP NOT
TO SCALE

HEATH LANE

ACKNOWLEDGEMENTS
We would like to thank all those people who have helped in any way towards the compiling of this publication - especially Martyn Jamieson, the Senior Area Ranger at Thurstaston; Bernard McLinden,Countryside Ranger at Hadlow Road Station and members of the Merseyside Railway History Group - Charlie Heywood, Harry Leadbetter and Ted Lloyd.

BIBLIOGRAPHY
Walking the Wirral Way   John Williams 1981
The Hooton to West Kirby Branch Line and the Wirral Way
                                  Merseyside Railway History Group 1982
Neston and Parkgate   Jeffrey Pearson 1985
Railway Stations of Wirral   Merseyside Railway History Group 1994
Pamphlets, guides etc. on the Wirral way   Cheshire County Council
Pamphlets, guides etc. on the Wirral way   Wirral Borough Council

PUBLICATIONS
By the Same Authors:
Yesterday's Wirral No 1 - Neston, Parkgate & Heswall
Yesterday's Wirral No 2 - Birkenhead, Prenton & Oxton
Yesterday's Wirral No 3 - West Kirby & Hoylake
Yesterday's Wirral No 4 - Wallasey & New Brighton
Yesterday's Wirral No 5 - Wallasey, New Brighton & Moreton
Yesterday's Wirral No 6 - Neston, Parkgate & Heswall including Thurstaston & Irby
Yesterday's Wirral No 7 - Birkenhead, Oxton & Prenton including Bidston & Upton
Yesterday's Wirral No 8 - Bebington & the Mid Wirral Villages
Birkenhead, A Pictorial History - over 180 photographs in and around Birkenhead

By the Same Publishers:
The Funny Side of Wirral	Cartoons by Bill Stott
Another Funny Side of Wirral	Cartoons by Bill Stott
Liverpool	Cartoons by Bill Stott
Shadow to Shadow	History of Bristol Aeroplane Banwell & BAJ
Birkenhead Electric Trams	Charles Rycroft
The Birkenhead Bus	TB Maund
The Wallasey Bus	TB Maund
Murder & Mayhem in Birkenhead	David Malcolm
Railway Stations of Wirral	Merseyside Railway History Group

Any of the above publications may be purchased - Post Free in the UK or Postage at cost abroad - direct from the publishers (if available), address on page one.